Life in a forest

Haugen, Hayley M Test#: 85926

Points: 1.0 Lvl: 7.6

ECOSYSTEMS

Life in a
Forest

Hayley Mitchell Haugen

KIDHAVEN PRESS

An imprint of Thomson Gale, a part of The Thomson Corporation

THOMSON

GALE

Detroit • New York • San Francisco • San Diego • New Haven, Conn. • Waterville, Maine • London • Munich

For more information, contact
KidHaven Press
27500 Drake Rd.
Farmington Hills, MI 48331-3535
Or you can visit our Internet site at http://www.gale.com

LIBRARY OF CONGRESS CATALOGING-IN-PUBLICATION DATA

Haugen, Hayley Mitchell, 1968–
Life in a forest / by Hayley Mitchell Haugen.
    p. cm. — (Ecosystems)
Includes bibliographical references (p.).
Contents: What is a forest?—Forest trees and plants—Forest wildlife—Threats to the forest.
  ISBN 0-7377-3080-3 (hard cover : alk. paper)
  1. Forest ecology—Juvenile literature. 2. Forests and forestry—Juvenile literature.
I. Title. II. Series.
  QH541.5.F6H38 2005
  577.3—dc22

2004018198

Printed in the United States of America

Contents

Chapter 1

What Is a Forest?

Standing outside a forest for the first time, visitors might describe the woods simply as a large area of land covered with lots of trees. It is true that it takes many trees to make a forest, but the forest environment also abounds with a great variety of plants, shrubs, and flowers, as well as numerous animals, birds, and insects. Interacting together, these trees, plants, and animal species make up the forest **ecosystem**.

Today, about 30 percent of Earth's land areas are covered in forests. There are six different kinds of forests. They are tropical rain forests, tropical seasonal forests, two types of **temperate forests**, **boreal forests**, and savannas. The largest tropical rain forests grow in the Amazon of South America, the Congo of Africa, and throughout Southeast Asia. Unlike tropical rain forests, which are wet all the time, tropical seasonal forests have both wet and dry seasons. These forests are located in parts of Central and South America, Africa, India, China, and Australia.

The Earth's forests provide habitat for many animals, such as this doe and her two fawns.

North America, western Europe, and eastern Asia all have warm summers and cold winters. This temperate, or mild, climate supports the growth of temperate **deciduous** forests. Deciduous trees have broad, flat leaves that fall off in the winter and grow back in the spring. In other temperate forests, **evergreen** trees grow. Evergreen trees remain green all year long because the leaves or needles they shed are replaced throughout the year. These temperate evergreen forests especially thrive in coastal areas. They are found on the northwest coast of North America, the south coast of Chile, the west coast of New Zealand, and the southeast coast of Australia.

Boreal forests and savannas are the last two types of forests. They are very different from one another. The word *boreal* means northern. Boreal forests are located in regions in northern Europe, Asia, and North America that have extremely cold winters and short summers. Savannas are located in places with low rainfall and poor soil. Because this environment limits tree growth, in savannas trees are widely spaced, instead of densely packed together, as in other forests. Central America, Africa, India, Southeast Asia, and Australia all include terrain with savannas.

American Forests

Only about 16 percent of the world's forests are located in the United States, but forests in America still cover more than 700 million acres (283.3 million hectares). Spread throughout the country,

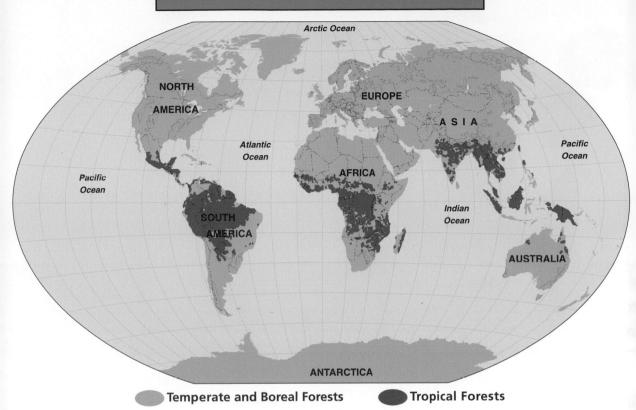

Forests of the World

Arctic Ocean

NORTH
AMERICA

EUROPE

ASIA

Atlantic
Ocean

Pacific
Ocean

Pacific
Ocean

AFRICA

SOUTH
AMERICA

Indian
Ocean

AUSTRALIA

ANTARCTICA

○ Temperate and Boreal Forests   ● Tropical Forests

these millions of acres of forests occupy about one-third of America's total land. Because the climates and landscapes of the fifty states vary so greatly, five of the six different types of forests grow in the United States. Tropical rain forests are the only type of forest that do not grow here.

Among the different kinds of forests in America, the temperate and boreal forests are the most typical. With warm, wet summers and cold winters, temperate forests are neither extremely hot nor extremely cold. Boreal forests, however, grow in America's coldest

regions, where the trees have a much shorter growing season.

Most temperate forests in the United States consist of deciduous trees, but some also contain evergreens. Temperate forests with deciduous trees can be found

Each fall, as the green chlorophyll disappears from the leaves of deciduous trees, bright shades of red, orange, and yellow are revealed.

east of the Mississippi River, extending northward into the northern states of the Great Lakes. The temperature in these forests ranges from 50 to 70 degrees Fahrenheit (10 to 21 degrees Celsius). The average rainfall is 30 to 80 inches (76 to 203cm) a year.

As the seasons change from summer to fall each year, the bright red, orange, and yellow leaves of the deciduous trees turn the temperate forest into an artist's palette of color. One often-forgotten fact is that these colors are actually present in the leaves all along. These colors are simply covered by the green pigment in **chlorophyll** during the rest of the year. In the fall, trees grow an extra layer of cells between the tree branch and leaf stem. Called the **abscission layer**, these cells cut off the leaves' supply of water and nutrients and prevent further leaf production. The green chlorophyll then disappears from the leaf, revealing the vibrant colors underneath.

The deciduous trees of the temperate forests could not survive the harsh winter conditions in the boreal forest. Boreal forests are found in the northernmost regions of North America. The winters in boreal forests last up to eight months. With temperatures dropping below –94 degrees Fahrenheit (–70 degrees Celsius), these winters are extremely cold and produce heavy snowfall. Because of the long winters, the growing season for trees and other plants in the boreal forest lasts only three months in the summer.

An eagle soars above spruce trees in an Alaskan boreal forest. Spruce trees, like all conifers, grow needles (inset) and produce cones (right).

However, heavy rains and extended daylight hours during the summer months are ideal conditions for the boreal **conifers** (evergreen trees that produce cones) to grow. Conifers are found in Minnesota, Wisconsin, and Michigan, for example, which are known for their eastern white pine and red pine trees. In the winter, the waxy outer coating of the conifers' needles helps protect these trees from water loss in freezing temperatures.

The Importance of Forests

Whether temperate, boreal, tropical, or savanna, the world's forests play a number of important roles.

A young Virginia opossum makes itself at home in this pine tree.

First, forests are important for the environment. The trees and other plant life of the forest provide **habitat** for numerous animal, insect, and bird species. Many of these species would die out without the support of their forest ecosystem. In addition to providing plant and animal habitat, the trees of the forest also produce oxygen for both animals and humans.

Humans also turn to forests for the production of many products they use every day. Wood from forests is used as lumber and plywood in the construction of houses and furniture. It is also processed into other products, including paper, plastics, some fibers, and a variety of waxes and oils.

In addition to the many products that come from forests, forests offer a place for recreation and relaxation. Thousands of people go to forests each year to camp, hike, ski, and hunt.

Visiting the Pacific Coastal Forests

Some of the most often visited temperate forests in the world are found along the Pacific coast from central California to southern Oregon. The mild, wet winters and dry summers on the Pacific coast especially encourage the growth of conifers within these temperate forests.

The redwood forests of northern California are coniferous forests that are a favorite attraction for vacationers. The redwoods and giant sequoias in this region are the oldest and largest living trees on

These giant sequoias tower high above a hiker standing on the forest floor.

Earth. Towering more than 350 feet (106.7m) above the forest floor, the giant sequoias can weigh in at more than 6,000 tons (5,443 metric tons). Some bristlecone pines in the area are more than 5,000 years old.

America's redwoods and sequoias are famous worldwide for their age and size, and the deciduous forests are famous for their fall foliage. In many ways, however, these famous forests are just like America's less famous ones. Forests are all made up of interesting layers of trees and plants that offer much for visitors to see and learn about the forest ecosystem.

Chapter 2

Forest Trees and Plants

Whether it is a subtropical forest along the hot and humid Atlantic coast, or an awe-inspiring redwood forest of the Pacific Northwest, every forest is made up of different strata, or layers, of plants. In a city, concrete, glass, and lumber combine to form skyscrapers that hover one above the other as they stretch to the clouds. Of course, the building materials for the different strata of a forest are much different from those of a city. But the towering effect is much the same for forest trees as it is for skyscrapers.

The Canopy and Understory

Whereas cities are built by layers of man-made materials, forests are built by layers of trees and other

Layers of a Forest

Canopy and Understory

The canopy contains the oldest and tallest trees, and the understory contains shorter trees and saplings. Birds and insects call these layers home.

Shrub and Herb Layers

In this layer grow the woody shrubs, berry bushes, ferns, wildflowers, and grasses. Birds, insects, and ground-dwelling animals—such as snakes, mice, foxes, and bears—can be found here.

Forest Floor

Dead leaves, moss, lichen, and rotting wood cover the forest floor. Insects, spiders, worms, and soil bacteria live here.

plant life. Scientists divide forests into five different layers. These are **canopy**, **understory**, shrub layer, herb layer, and forest floor. The first strata, the canopy, is made up of the oldest, tallest, and most common (or most dominant) trees in a forest. The dense leaves and branches of the tops of these trees often join together to form a canopy of shade over the other layers below.

In the canopy layer of the temperate forest, dominant trees can grow up to 100 feet (30.48m) in height. They vary greatly from region to region. In the central Appalachian Mountain region, for example, the dominant trees include ash, beech, sugar maple, and different kinds of oak. Beech and sugar maple trees dominate in the Northeast. Basswood and maple dominate in temperate forests in the northwestern states.

Below the forest canopy is the understory. The understory is made up of younger trees, called saplings, and other trees that are shorter than the canopy trees. These trees are unlikely to grow to the great heights of the canopy trees because the canopy limits the amount of sunlight they receive. In the United States, the understory layer might include trees such as black cherry, red maple, and white elm. In some forests, the understory includes flowering trees, such as the dogwoods common to the southern Appalachian forests.

The Shrub and Herb Layers

The next layer of the forest, the shrub layer, gets even less sunlight than the understory. Because

Bushy rhododendrons fill out the shrub layer of this forest in Oregon.

forests with thick canopy and understory layers do not get much sunlight, the shrub layer does not usually grow very thick. As its name suggests, this layer consists of shrubs. Shrubs grow much closer to the ground than trees do, are bushy in appearance, and consist of more than one woody stem.

Bushy shrubs such as rhododendrons grow along the northern coast of California. Huckleberry shrubs growing in the Idaho Panhandle National Forest are a favorite attraction for visitors, who come to pick the berries. Along with the trees and plants of the canopy and understory layers, these shrubs and many others provide habitat for numerous forest birds and insects.

The fourth layer of the forest is the herb layer. The herb layer is made up of soft-stemmed plants, including many different kinds of wildflowers and ferns, grasses, herbs, and tree seedlings. In the Clearwater National Forest in Idaho, the herb layer consists

Ferns, grasses, and other soft-stemmed plants make up the forest's herb layer.

of more than twenty varieties of ferns in addition to the other plants that provide habitat for the forest's ground-dwelling animals. Small animals, such as snakes, turtles, and mice, and larger animals, such as deer and bear, can be found in the herb layer.

The Dark, Damp Forest Floor

One final layer of the forest lies beneath the herb layer. This layer is the forest floor. The forest floor is covered with twigs, rotting leaves, and tree branches that have fallen from the higher layers. Earthworms, spiders, **fungi**, and bacteria all mingle in this darkest, dampest layer of the forest.

The dominant trees of the forest canopy tower magnificently over all life in the forest. However, these trees could not grow without the help of the organisms living far below on the forest floor. Bacteria, fungi, insects, and worms all aid the ecosystem by eating the waste that litters the forest floor. This waste includes rotting leaves, animal droppings, and dead animals.

As the organisms on the forest floor eat away at this waste, it becomes smaller. This process is called the **decomposition** process. The decomposition process is ongoing and returns beneficial nutrients to the forest soil. These nutrients, including nitrogen, phosphorus, and potassium, are then absorbed into the roots of trees and plants and help ensure the future growth of the forest.

Trees in the Boreal Forest

Temperate forests can support a wide variety of trees and other plant life within their various strata. Because of harsh weather, however, the structure of the boreal forests is much simpler. Rather than having a canopy and understory, boreal forests such as those in northern Minnesota, Wisconsin, and Michigan have only one layer of trees. Trees most commonly found in boreal forests include evergreen conifers such as balsam fir, black and white spruce varieties, and jack pine. These trees grow up to 75 feet (22.86m) in height.

Fungi and mosses, like those growing at the foot of this birch tree, thrive on the damp forest floor.

Black spruce trees are one of the few tree species commonly found in boreal forests.

The topsoil in boreal forests is usually sandy and unable to support the herbs, shrubs, and other small plants found in the temperate forest. Mosses and lichens are common in the boreal forest, however. They form a thick layer on the forest floor and also grow on tree trunks and branches throughout the boreal forest. The boreal forest does not support as large a variety of trees and plant life as the temperate forest does. Like the temperate forest, however, it provides essential habitat for various animal, bird, and insect species.

Chapter 3

Forest Wildlife

Just as various trees and plants make up the different layers of the forest, different birds, animals, and insects make use of the various forest layers for food, water, and shelter. Since the trees that make up the canopy and understory layers receive the most sunlight, these layers produce more food than the others. Birds, insects, and animals that eat fruit, nuts, and leaves spend most of their time in the canopy and understory.

Birds occupy more layers of the temperate forest than most other animals do. Yellow-throated vireos and hundreds of other bird species live in the canopy and understory. One layer below the understory, the shrub layer is a favorite nesting spot for

23

The scarlet tanager is just one of the hundreds of bird species that live in the forest.

hooded warblers and many other birds. Some birds, such as ovenbirds and winter wrens, do not live in trees at all. These birds prefer to build covered nests on the forest floor.

Living on the Forest Floor

Abounding in an endless maze of nooks and crannies, the underbrush, leaf piles, and fallen trees collecting on the forest floor attract many small creatures of the forest. Mice, opossums, raccoons, and squirrels are just a few of the small mammals that spend much of their time on the forest floor. Chipmunks are also common in the forest, but they are rarely seen in the summer months.

Despite the shade from the trees, summer in the forest is too hot for chipmunks and some other small mammals. To prevent overheating and becoming dehydrated, the chipmunk burrows underground in the summer. It sleeps there for many days, sometimes even weeks at a time. This practice of burrowing underground and sleeping is called estivation.

Squirrels and other small mammals spend much of their time foraging for food on the forest floor.

Though some of the forest's small animals may sleep through the summer, the forest's larger animal species remain active. Bears, bobcats, foxes, and wild boars live in America's temperate forests year-round. Moose, elk, and white-tailed deer are also common.

While most animals have a role in maintaining the health of the forest ecosystem, some do more harm than good. The porcupine is one of these. Porcupines are very destructive creatures. They girdle trees, which means they chew through the bark all around a tree. They chew deep enough to stop the flow of food between a tree and its roots, which kills the tree. Each year porcupines kill ponderosa pines

Bobcats prowl through America's temperate forests year-round.

in the Pacific Northwest and northern hardwoods in the Great Lakes states and New England forests.

In addition to mammals such as the porcupine, the forest ecosystem also supports a number of reptiles and amphibians. Box turtles found in the forest can live up to one hundred years, and they live their entire lives on land. They move slowly along the forest floor, eating berries, seeds, mushrooms, and insects. In the winter, they burrow as far as 2 feet (0.6m) down into the soil to keep warm. Gray tree frogs, red-backed salamanders, and garter snakes are also common in America's forests.

Insects in the Forest

From the tallest treetop to the damp soil on the forest floor, thousands of insects also make their home in the forest. These insects are a food source for many forest birds and animals, and many also support the growth of the forest by helping to pollinate wildflowers. Bees, wasps, butterflies, and beetles, for example, are all pollinators.

While many insects play a productive role in the forest ecosystem, others play a destructive role by attacking plants and trees. In 1998, 54 million acres (21.9 million hectares) of forest in the United States were affected by seven kinds of disease-causing insects. Aphids and cicadas, for instance, attack both the leaves and the stems, sucking the sap from trees. Other insects, such as weevils, termites, and wireworms, attack the roots of small trees.

Bark beetles are especially damaging to trees. These beetles burrow into tree trunks and large branches. As they burrow, they leave behind a blue stain fungus that slowly kills the trees. The mountain pine beetle is one of the most destructive kinds of bark beetles. Mountain pine beetles have destroyed thousands of acres of lodgepole and western white pine in the western United States. They have also been destructive to ponderosa pine in the Black Hills and Rocky Mountains.

Animals in the Boreal Forest

Although the boreal forest does not support as many layers of trees and plant life as the temperate forest, it still provides habitat for numerous birds and other animals. For example, the boreal forest especially attracts a number of bird species that nest in needleleaf trees such as firs and pines. These birds include the gray jay, red-breasted nuthatch, and winter wren. The boreal forest also hosts ducks, loons, owls, and woodpeckers.

Small animals of the boreal forest include beavers, mice, and snowshoe hares. Larger animals of the boreal forest include bears, caribou, deer, and moose. Even through the long winter, many of these animals forage for food in the forest. In the coldest months, shrews, mice, and other small animals burrow deep under the snow for warmth. Others nest deep inside holes in trees, where they seek protection from the harsh climate.

Caribou can survive even the harshest winters in the boreal forest.

Some animals simply sleep until spring. The black bears of the boreal forest, for example, retreat to caves and hibernate through the winter. During hibernation, a bear's body temperature drops and it breathes much more slowly than normal. Expending much less energy in this way, the black bear is able to live off the body fat it has stored throughout the year, and has no need for food or water for many months.

High in the northern Rocky Mountains, grizzly bears seek out supplies of whitebark pine nuts before they hibernate. The nuts are easy to collect because ground squirrels and a bird called the Clark's nutcracker gather the nuts and bury them throughout the forest. These nuts are especially important to the grizzlies because they contribute to up to 40 percent of the bears' diet and help them build up their fat before their winter sleep. In addition to the grizzly bears, the Clark's nutcracker, and ground squirrels, more than 110 other wildlife species depend on the nut and seed crops from the whitebark pine trees.

Without an ample supply of nuts from the whitebark pine, the Rocky Mountain grizzly bears could not hibernate safely through the winter; they also depend on the stable forest environment for the availability of nuts and other food when they wake up hungry in the spring. However, a stable forest habitat is not guaranteed for any of the forest species. At one time, for example, wolves could be found in America's temperate and boreal forests

Grizzly bears eat lots of high-fat pine nuts in the fall before they bed down for their long winter sleep.

year-round, but they are not as common today as in the past. They are just one of a number of forest animals that have become endangered due to the effects of overhunting and the clearing of their forest habitat for use by people.

Chapter 4

Threats to the Forest

Forests worldwide face a variety of threats. Some result from acts of nature, such as floods and droughts. The more common threats to forests, however, are caused by people.

Deforestation

The destruction of forests is commonly referred to as **deforestation**. About 300 years ago, forests covered half of the land in the United States. Today, only about one-third of America's land supports forests. Much of the previously forested land in the United States has been cleared for farming or development of cities. The steady growth of cities also increases air pollution, another threat to the forest environment.

Most of this air pollution comes from factories, power plants, and cars. Through their burning of oil, coal, and gas, city factories and power plants often release poisonous gases into the air. Automobile emissions in congested cities are also a form of air pollution.

When the pollutants from factories and cars combine with rain or other precipitation in the atmosphere, they may fall back to Earth as **acid rain**. Chemicals in the acid rain seep into the soil in forests and damage the root systems of trees and plants. Unable to absorb the nutrients they need to grow, trees and plants die. This is happening in Pennsylvania, where researchers say thousands of acres of forests are being damaged by acid rain.

Deforestation is harmful because it reduces habitat for animals and contributes to soil erosion.

Cutting and Burning Trees

In addition to air pollution, human cutting and burning of forests is another main cause of deforestation. Forests are cleared for a number of reasons. For example, forests in the United States, Canada, and countries of the former Soviet Union supply more than half the world's industrial lumber.

This lumber is used in the construction industry for buildings or in other industries, such as paper manufacturing. In the United States more than 19 million board feet (66,120 cubic meters) of softwood lumber was used in 2003 for the construction of housing. Worldwide, more than 12 percent of the lumber from the world's forests is used for making paper. By the year 2050, more than 3 billion trees will be cut down and processed just to keep up with the world's need for toilet paper.

Cut from a Canadian forest, this lumber will be used to construct buildings and to make paper.

With so many trees lost to these industries each year, forest conservationists worry about the future of the forests. They argue that the lumber and manufacturing industries need to do more to ensure that forests remain sustainable. This means that although forest resources can be used by people, the forest habitat should not be permanently damaged in the process.

Shrinking Forests

Each year, many animal and plant species are lost to the effects of deforestation. The loss of forests also creates ecological problems that affect life for people, animals, and plants outside the forest environment. For example, forests help counter the effects of heavy rains. The soil in forests is bound to the roots of the trees. The binding of roots and soil helps trap rainwater within the forest.

When trees are cleared for lumber or destroyed by fire, the soil erodes and it is unable to hold large amounts of water. Usually, the forest releases these stores of rainwater slowly into streams and rivers. When the forest shrinks and can no longer hold the water, flooding results.

In 2004, floods killed more than 3,800 people in the Caribbean island nation of Haiti. The unusually heavy rains that led to the flooding resulted from Hurricane Jeanne. While flooding is often a problem wherever a hurricane hits, Haiti's problems were made worse by deforestation. Ninety-eight percent of Haiti's forests have been cut down for fuel and housing.

Stripped of trees, the land has little topsoil remaining to hold water from heavy rains like those that occurred during Hurricane Jeanne.

Forests Help Prevent Global Warming

Forests help prevent flooding, and they also help prevent **global warming**. Forest trees and plants produce oxygen through the process of **photosynthesis**. During photosynthesis, trees and plants harness the Sun's energy to make oxygen out of water and carbon dioxide absorbed from the atmosphere. The leaves in the forest then release water vapor, which helps keep the forest and nearby areas cool.

When trees are cleared from the forest, fewer trees go through the process of photosynthesis. This leaves more carbon dioxide than usual in the atmosphere, and less of the Sun's intense heat is reflected back into space by water vapor. Instead, the heat from the Sun is trapped near the surface of Earth by carbon dioxide and other gases.

Many scientists believe that the effect of this trapped heat, which they call the greenhouse effect, is contributing to the steady warming of the planet. They fear that Earth's increasing temperatures may eventually lead to devastating weather conditions, such as large-scale flooding from melting ice caps.

To help prevent global warming caused by the greenhouse effect, some researchers have suggested planting new trees in forests when others are cut

How Photosynthesis Works

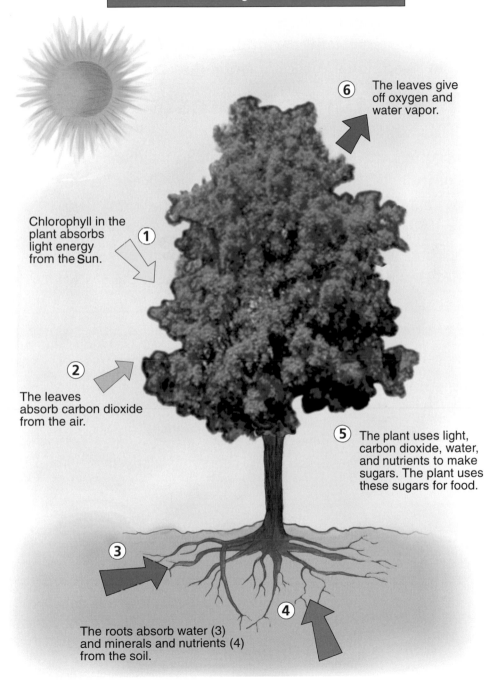

6 The leaves give off oxygen and water vapor.

1 Chlorophyll in the plant absorbs light energy from the Sun.

2 The leaves absorb carbon dioxide from the air.

5 The plant uses light, carbon dioxide, water, and nutrients to make sugars. The plant uses these sugars for food.

3 **4** The roots absorb water (3) and minerals and nutrients (4) from the soil.

down or burned for human use. While this plan may help over time, most scientists recommend limiting cutting and burning in the future. Burning forests is especially harmful, as burning wood releases additional carbon dioxide into the air.

The Future of Forests

Biologists fear that many forest plants and animals will become extinct in the future if global warming is not controlled. These plants and animals will not be able to adapt to increased temperatures in the forest habitat. Controlling carbon dioxide levels in the atmosphere can help prevent this and can help ensure the healthy future of forest ecosystems around the world.

Glossary

abscission layer: A new layer of cells across the base of a leaf stem that grows each autumn, cutting off the supply of nutrients and causing the leaves of deciduous trees to fall.

acid rain: Precipitation with high levels of acid, which results from rain mixing with pollutants in the atmosphere.

boreal forests: Forests located in colder, northern regions.

canopy: The topmost layer of the forest, which provides shade for the forest environment.

chlorophyll: The green chemical in plants that helps change water and carbon dioxide into energy for the plant.

conifers: Evergreen trees that usually produce cones.

deciduous: A tree that loses its leaves each year.

decomposition: The process by which bacteria and other organisms break down dead plants and animals to release the organic materials they contain.

deforestation: The destruction of forest trees and plants.

ecosystem: The environment in which plants and animals live together.

evergreen: A tree that keeps its leaves year-round.

fungi: Plantlike organisms that get nutrients by helping other plants decompose.

global warming: A change in the composition of gases in the air that causes the gradual warming of Earth's surface.

habitat: The home of a particular plant or animal.

photosynthesis: The process by which plants use sunlight to make oxygen out of water and carbon dioxide.

temperate forests: Forests found in a mild or moderate climate.

understory: The second layer of trees that stands just beneath the canopy in a forest.

For Further Exploration

Books

Melvin Berger and Michael Rothman, *Does It Always Rain in the Rainforest?* New York: Scholastic, 2002. Authors Berger and Rothman answer more than 75 questions about tropical rain forests. They cover everything from Brazilian nut trees and giant vines to hummingbirds and anteaters. Colorful illustrations provide a glimpse of what life is like in a tropical rain forest.

Nic Bishop, *Forest Explorer: A Life-Size Field Guide.* New York: Scholastic, 2004. This photo-filled book depicts several different deciduous forest habitats. It includes field notes about the insects and animals shown, as well as tips on how to explore a real forest.

Jane Drake, *Forestry.* Toronto, Ontario: Kids Can Press, 2002. In this text, young readers are introduced to Cameron and his uncle, who describe the felling, harvesting, and replanting of forest trees.

Anita Ganeri, *Habitats: Forests.* East Sussex, England: Wayland, 1996. The color photographs and text of this book tell the story of forests world-

41

wide. Forest animals, plants, and people are described in detail.

Elizabeth Kaplan, *Temperate Forest.* Tarrytown, NY: Benchmark Books, 1996. This book describes the history of temperate forests, shows the temperate forest through the seasons, and discusses a number of threats to temperate forests.

Donna Loughran, *Living in the Forest.* New York: Childrens Press, 2003. This book describes how people make their homes in or near the forests and how their lives are affected by the forest environment.

Edward Parker, *Forests for the Future.* Chatham, NJ: Raintree Steck-Vaughn, 1998. This colorfully illustrated book describes many different kinds of forests and the roles they play in both natural and human environments. It discusses numerous threats to forests and ways to save forests for the future.

Dorothy Hinshaw Patent, *Garden of the Spirit Bear: Life in the Great Northern Rainforest.* New York: Houghton Mifflin, 2004. Noted naturalist Dorothy Hinshaw Patent describes the elusive spirit bear and its home, which is in danger of being destroyed by loggers and settlers as they clear-cut the ancient Canadian forests for lumber.

Laurence Pringle, *Fire in the Forest: A Cycle of Growth and Renewal.* New York: Simon & Schuster, 1995. A number of realistic paintings in this book illustrate the forest landscape before, during, and after a fire. Rather than focusing on the destructive nature of fire, this text describes the positive effects of fires in forest habitats.

April Pulley Sayre, *Temperate Deciduous Forest*. New York: Twenty-First Century Books, 1994. Topics in this book include descriptions of the climate and geology of temperate deciduous forests. Temperate forest plants, animals, and human communities are discussed in detail.

Frank Staub, *America's Forests*. Minneapolis: Carolrhoda Books, 1999. This book takes a look at American forests from coast to coast. It provides specific details about the kinds of trees and animals found in forests and explains how America's forests have changed over time.

Web Sites

Explore the Fantastic Forest, National Geographic Kids (www.nationalgeographic.com/forest). At this site sponsored by *National Geographic*, kids can explore a variety of plant and animal habitats found in the forest.

Smokey Kids, SmokeyBear.com (www. smokeybear. com/kids/default.asp). The special kids' section on Smokey's site offers games, stories, and educational material for young readers, describing Smokey's rules for forest fire safety and prevention.

USDA for Kids (www.usda.gov/news/usdakids). This colorful site includes links to Woodsy Owl, Natural Resource Conservation Education, Backyard Conservation, Nature Watch, and much more.

World Wildlife Fund (www.worldwildlife. org/index.cfm). The World Wildlife Fund leads international efforts to protect endangered species and their habitats. This Web site offers educational materials, games, and quizzes for children and adults.

Index

45

Picture Credits

About the Author

Hayley Mitchell Haugen holds master's degrees in English and creative writing, and she is currently working on her PhD in American literature at Ohio University. She teaches creative writing and composition at the college level and has written numerous nonfiction books for teens and children published by Greenhaven Press, Lucent Books, and KidHaven Press.